SEPPUKU QUARTERLY

SEPPUKU QUARTERLY

Seppuku Quarterly/Joseph Fulkerson
ISBN: 978-1-7371509-1-6
Laughing Ronin Press

www.LaughingRoninPress.com

Notes from the Editor

sep·pu·ku /ˈsepo͞oˌko͞o, səˈpo͞oˌko͞o/
(Japanese: 切腹, "cutting [the] belly") sometimes referred to as ***harakiri*** is a form of Japanese ritual suicide by disembowelment.

It was favored under Bushidō (warrior code) as an effective way to demonstrate the courage, self-control, and strong resolve of the samurai and to prove sincerity of purpose.

I've always been fascinated by the image this word invokes. That one would live and die by their honor. It is rare for someone to stand by their word nowadays, and unfathomable to commit oneself to death to ensure honor is maintained or reinstated.

It is my express purpose to fill the pages of this journal with writing that reflects, demonstrates, and embodies these qualities. To celebrate authenticity. To challenge the status quo. To have the strength to build bridges when possible and burn them down when necessary.

To that end, I believe I have found success.

Thank you to all that contributed to this inaugural issue of Seppuku Quarterly journal, and to those that will do so in future iterations.

Humbly,
Joseph Fulkerson

UFO Motel

Paul Cordeiro

Buzzards are swimming
in oil puddles
left behind by
adulterer's junkers.
As Mrs. so and so enters
the gift shop for a potted cactus,
maybe a western state thimble
for a dust-caked collection,
I'm hallucinating the buzzards
and as dehydrated as a tourist
with jet lag, who
sometimes dries out
flying from East to West.
I steer the white sedan rental
out of the UFO motel
parking lot.
Its aluminum dome-shaped

roof, like a flying saucer

for snow to slide off,

glints.

Librarian, Ex-Wife

Paul Cordeiro

She wouldn't wear

a crucifix

between her small breasts

even to a biker's wedding.

Classic

Tony Brewer

Every film and cartoon I watched as a kid
too young to get into a theatre alone
was heavily edited for network television
The ceaseless blasting of Daffy Duck's face off
remained but the bull never exploded
The suicide bear only aired once that I saw

All the light T&A commercial broken
and cussing badly dubbed because
you couldn't say fuck and 6 other things
Sex was always off screen
Phoebe Cates out of the pool
never happened from the neck down
James Bond was merely salacious
like Pepe Le Pew
The girl in the after school special who had sex
for money learned a valuable lesson and went home
unlike rings busted on the news
Even *The Omen* on Sunday night

left the unavoidable train sandwich

to the imagination – frames excised

to fit the prime time slot

Layers of mediated experience

flayed apart by letterboxed director's cuts

smearing screens in undiluted gore

when I thought I had seen it all

Taxi Driver 4pm on Saturday afternoon

minus the slow dance with her pimp

Apocalypse Now! whittled down to 2.5 hours

Warner Bros. witch doctors with nose bones stayed

but enough violence cut

to make Bugs Bunny less cruel or cool

My imagination was rated R

protected from the un-reality of art

while the news filled the margins with a curated narrative and enough space

for a word from our sponsors

Damn Broke

Tony Brewer

Back when the river flowed
I wrote all night to weather a flood
When it stopped it snowed
Mist over water and mud

I wrote all night to weather a flood
The cards turned in my favor
Mist over water and mud
Buried a human labor

The cards turned in my favor
Lost in nonsense scales
Buried a human labor
Mercy the sun entails

Lost in nonsense scales
Good work in better places

Mercy the sun entails

Making wild faces

Good work in better places

When it stopped it snowed

Making wild faces

Back when the river flowed

On Being An Outlaw Poet

Ron Whitehead

"To live outside the law you must be honest."

--Bob Dylan, Outlaw Poet

"An outlaw can be defined as somebody who lives outside the law, beyond the law, not necessarily against it. By the time I wrote Hell's Angels I was riding with them and it was clear that it was no longer possible for me to go back and live within the law...

There were a lot more outlaws than me. I was just a writer. I wasn't trying to be an outlaw writer. I never heard of the term, somebody else made it up. But we were all outside the law, Kerouac, Miller, Burroughs, Ginsberg, Kesey, me. I didn't have a gauge as to who was the worst outlaw. I just recognized my allies, my people."

--Hunter S. Thompson, Outlaw Writer

The Ending of Time, An Alchemical Rant

Ron Whitehead

"time was, time is, time will be no more"

and it's the big bang epiphany

in the gap between thought and image

voices   streams racing

whispering through my blood

pleading through my bones

strange activities of my nerves

the unconscious life of the mind

a tetrameter of iambs marching

shouting

alchemically trans mutative symbol

decipherment

the book as sacred elixir

manger du livre

eat the book

and the words

will set you free

"the shortest distance between two points
is creative distance"

and Allen Ginsberg howls
"i saw the best minds of my generation
destroyed by
madness, starving, hysterical naked"

and Diane di Prima rants
"the only war that matters is the war against
the
imagination all other wars are subsumed in
it"

and Amiri Baraka chants
"they have turned, and say that i am dying.
that
i have thrown
my life
away. they
have left me alone, where
there is no one, nothing

save who i am. not a note

not a word."

and Lawrence Ferlinghetti paints

pictures of the gone world

mysterium tremendum gnostical turpitude

Allen Ginsberg   Diane di Prima

Amiri Baraka   Lawrence Ferlinghetti

numinous howls and rants and chants and

paintings

and years of tears come fiercely flowing

streaming

all the pain   wells up

years of failure   of not being enough for

anyone

years of wandering   lost   on the outside

outlaw

being told "you ain't shit   you don't fit   what

the

fuck you doin here?   all you've done is
create pain and sorrow
wouldn't you be better off dead?"

turning away from walking away from
disappearing from
bullies authorities tyrants the past the dead
in the hermetic corridors of authority the
dead
somberly splash in their shallow sewers
devouring and regurgitating themselves
and with tears in my eyes a snarl on my lips
and
peace in my heart
i'm failing as no other dare fail

and i'm in the gap between thought and
image
how'd i get here after all the years
of not being self
after all the years of being   other
of floating out of my body   on the ceiling

watching skin blood bones nerves going

through the motions

believing in space and time without realizing

i was already

out   out of sync   beyond chaos

breathing rhythms at the ending of time

and now here in the gap between thought

and image

where the only distance is creative distance

here now   at the ending of time

i focus all three eyes in wolf fashion

closing time

i walk through the stone called lump of fat

and i float through the fire that is central

and i enter the upper chamber of the golden

pyramid

the confluence of all streams

polyglot commingling of all voices

thalass feeds herself

and as i float over the open sarcophagus

i am

the ocean of consciousness

Screaming Into the Night

Joseph Fulkerson

Sometimes
writing feels like
screaming
into the black
of night
with a bullhorn

other times
it feels like whispering
a secret into the ear
of your sweetheart

either way

words are strung together
to form sentences

which form paragraphs
and chapters

in much the same way
they always have

but on the rare occasion
when the stars align
and the muse takes pity

new and exciting ways
are found
to say those things
which can't be
easily expressed

and that is what
keeps me
coming back
to the page.

Volcano Tears

Joseph Fulkerson

A tear falls from
the cheek of a volcano
scorching the earth,
searing its emotions
into the footprint of history

Empath

Jonathan S Baker

After the deed is done

but before we have parted ways

she tells me that

she has something else to say,

and as badly as I want to be gone,

to go home and lick my wounds,

to move on, to learn and forget,

I say "okay" because I think

this is what an adult would do.

So I lay there blood pooling

belly full of buckshot

and I'm all ears for her monologue.

She tells me about the vast stores

of empathy she has,

about how she can feel others pain.

My vision is blurring

and she sounds so far away,

but wincing I agree through gritted teeth.

Then she causally steps her heel

onto the shining wetness

spreading across the front of my shirt

and says, "this is how I know

you're a narcissist

because I'm an empath

because you're a narcissist

because I'm an empath..."

Over and over droning on

until the words lose form

and become the deafening buzz

of some insects come

to feed on my carcass.

As she is casting a spell

that she learned from a magazine,

I have a moment of clarity.

In my own mind someone,

I think it's me, screams,

"Jesus Christ is she fucking with me?"

That shout, it gives me

the strength to get to my feet

and say a goodbye, to say anything

and I've got to leave.

But before I reach the door she says,

"My therapist agrees."

I pause ready to take the bait.

In my stupor this sounds almost sane.

I nearly turned away from the door

But I look at the frame

And see how everything I touch

is getting stained.

I fall through the door

and stumble away.

THE MANUFACTURER

Sam Pink

I watched a paper plate
propelled by wind
roll down the street
all the way out of view
and it made me want to
take over the world.

There are only:
the things I love
and
things I'd scrape from my boot
to step on again.
May I never step in it again.

Because I do believe it is time.
To see all as it is.
Time to climb a mountain.
Kill a dragon.
Fall in love.

Break bricks by blinking.
Time to step into the clear fire
which looks a lot like
the air right in front of you.

Victory in the form of
an ever-present tense.
No more costume changes
on the same dumb mannequin.
Flexing downward
and through clenched teeth
I say,
'Play your song, motherfucker.'

And all is well.

At first it takes years
to see what someone is about.
And then it takes seconds.
And then it takes what amounts to
seconds to those seconds
if those seconds were years.

And then you explode into dandelion fuzz.

Thinking your life is

what you safeguard so carefully

but knowing

the best parts have happened unguarded.

Flexing, a rainbow forms between my biceps

and I continue the journey.

And all is well.

30-some years of feedback

and then

the song starts.

Right, yeah.

Turning into my apartment parking lot

I saw a man on the sidewalk and

his bottom half was standing but

his top half was fully hunched-over asleep

almost touching his toes.

And I briefly perceived him as

having been powered down--

recalled to the manufacturer.

ANTI-SOCIAL MEDIA

Martin Appleby

I am sick of my phone
being the last thing I look at
before I go to sleep
and the first thing I look at
when I wake up
I am sick of my phone
distracting me
from anything that I do
I am addicted to
scrolling through the endless
timeline of nonsense
and bullshit
looking at adverts upon adverts
whilst I post adverts of my own
but as much as I may regret
ever getting a "smart" phone
- if I am being honest -
before I had one

I was only doing the same thing
but on a laptop instead
it is just now more accessible
now never leaves my side
now never leaves my mind
and if I had any sense
or the courage of my convictions
I would throw the thing into the sea
and retrain my brain
as the phone floats away
but I won't
I'll probably just finish this poem
and write a Tweet about it instead
and if this poem is ever published
I'll post a picture of it on Instagram
and share it on Facebook, too.
Fuck.

HARSH CRITIC

Martin Appleby

I found this writer on Instagram

who'd written a novel about punks

I like novels about punk

by punks

I looked it up on Amazon

(the antithesis of punk)

and the synopsis

was bloated and overwritten

full of every cliché about punk

they could squeeze in

Fuck that, I thought -

If the novel is as bad as the synopsis

then I'd sack it off before

finishing the first page -

and I realized what a pretentious

fucking prick I am.

As a writer myself -

who is yet to even finish

the first draft of any novel I have

ever started writing -

who the fuck am I to judge

someone who has actually

done the work and put themselves

out there into the world?

I followed the writer on Instagram

anyway

and the worst part is

that he never even followed me back.

Breathe

Isaac Hale

Clutch.

Shift. Clutch.

Twist. Lean...

Upright! BRAKE-CLUTCH-SHIFT.

Brake. Clutch. Shift.

Brake, mirrors...stop.

Train ahead. One hundred-five degrees asphalt
engines—heat radiating,

bleeding oil all over Camelback Road. Full stop.

Key, switch.

The oil smoke billows—no wind soaks up like
barbeque cooking,

choking, squinting, full stopping, breathing, gasping,
wet-leg oil leak.

Brand new pants gone down the drain 20 bucks.
Shoes a good excuse. No new shoes a good excuse.

Pack out, fag out, light out, light up, pack back.

Light back.

Choking, squinting, breathing. Full-stop.

“ding-ding-ding-ding...”

Key, switch, clutch-shift-kick...

Kick...KICK!

Clutch. Shift. clutch...twist.

Clutch. Shift. Twist.

Hold. Hold...

Clutch—clutch, twist...

Red mountain glides by 45 an hour barricades closer at 90, jagged Supes ridgeline ahead, breathe.

clutch.

shift.

twist!

Breathe

Some People Don't Belong Here

Isaac Hale

Some people don't belong here. They're a mistake. It's like something happened on the production line, somewhere in a factory. Somebody made a mistake and it resulted in a fucking person. Everybody freaked out, couldn't do shit about it. They try to cover it up.

They say *"Hi!"* to the person with big smiles on their faces and walk briskly away. They ask how the weekend was. They tell the guy they're proud of him.

Gotta make him feel like he'd been intended. Can't let him know what happened. Sometimes the weekend comes and goes so fast they forget his name. They wave and make a reference to a movie scene they saw one time, and let out a light chuckle. Lots of laughter happens during bad lies. (Crying only happens during the good ones.)

The person walks around asking some mundane questions, picking up a broom here and there – busy work. Sometimes he sees a window and glances out. There's trees and birds out there. A large parking lot, maybe. He asks some more questions. In the evening, the people go home. They eat and talk to their acquaintances on the phone. These days it is mostly text. They watch T.V. so they have something to talk about later.

The person goes home and walks around outside his house. This time he looks in the window. There might be a bed in there, or a refrigerator. A stray animal might walk up and act like a friend for a minute. It will likely pee if let inside. He pets it and shoos it away. When he goes inside he finds his own pee on the edge of the toilet seat.

Back at the factory, the engines are winding down. The lights are turned off. A screensaver is bouncing around the monitor. There's a glove on the assembly-line floor. It's quiet in the bathroom, good enough for sleeping.

Some people don't belong here. They are an accident. Someone made a mistake somewhere and a person happened.

Die Young

Dave Cullern

Every day
I stood privy
to long talks
in easy jobs
about future retirement
and waiting for the end

I watched
soft bellies
in soft chairs
wheel themselves
towards
discount biscuits
in old jars

I heard
the same words
on repeat
about the countdown
of someone else's life
as they travelled
the banal streets
of a town
they never left

and I couldn't help
but think
I'd rather die young
with a belly full of travels

and exotic disease,
unfed but free
with pockets filled with nothing
and a back crippled
by adventure

than spend a single day
melting in comfort
and forty year old dreams
with the cash to die
in a hole
deep enough
to rot in peace.

History Whispers

Dave Cullern

true beauty
is in the imperfections

the tiny moves
that remind us
of running in herds

the rough skin
that gives resistance
to our touch

the left alone hairs
of our fore bearers pores

so, in dreams,
when the street lights
shine true

we don't fuck
like they do in the movies

but why would we want to?

Haiku

Victor Clevenger

mighty no more
ashes of a large oak tree
scooped into small buckets

wet sand clinging
with each step of lovers' feet
the riverbanks widen

clover bursts in bloom
must be a good morning
two horses fuck in field

Tohm Bakelas

coldblooded prophets

speeding home I pass a turtle

holding the universe

inside its shell

distracted by everything

An egret glides overhead—

my watch is at home,

i wish for autumn

they know no laws

sparrows refuse adhering

to red traffic signals

they keep flying

Contributors

In order of appearance

Paul Cordeiro is a retired shoe salesman. Some of his verse appeared this year at **1870**, **Gasconade Review**, **Gray Sparrow Journal**, **Heroin Love Songs**, and **Sophisticated Chaos**. He also self-published a chapbook of haiku/ tanka, ***Wild Violets***, which is archived at The Haiku Foundation Digital Library. In Feb., **Analog Submission Press**, released a second limited-run chapbook of free verse, ***Do Not Touch.***

Tony Brewer is executive director of the spoken word stage at the 4th Street Arts Festival and his latest book is ***Homunculus*** (Dos Madres Press). He has been offering Poetry On Demand at coffeehouses, museums, cemeteries, churches, bars, and art and music festivals for over 10 years and he is one-third of the poetry performance group **Reservoir Dogwoods**. More at **tonybrewer71.blogspot.com**.

Ron Whitehead is a poet, writer, editor, publisher, professor, scholar, activist Ron Whitehead is the author of 24 books and 34 albums. In 1994 he wrote the poem "Never Give Up" with His Holiness The Dalai Lama. In 1996 he produced the Official Hunter S. Thompson Tribute featuring Hunter, his mother Virginia, his son Juan, Johnny Depp, Warren Zevon, Douglas Brinkley, David Amram, Roxanne Pulitzer, and many more. Ron has produced thousands of events and festivals, including 24 & 48 & 72 & 90 hour non-stop music & poetry Insomniacthons, in Europe and the USA. He has presented thousands of readings, talks, and performances around the world. He has edited and published hundreds of titles including works by President Jimmy Carter, His Holiness The Dalai Lama, Seamus Heaney, Wendell Berry, Allen Ginsberg, Jack Kerouac, William S. Burroughs, Lawrence Ferlinghetti, Rita Dove, Diane di Prima, Bono, John Updike, Douglas Brinkley, Jim Carroll, Anne Waldman, Joy Harjo, Yoko Ono, Robert Hunter, Amiri Baraka, Hunter S. Thompson, and numerous others. The recipient of many awards, his work has been translated into 20 languages. In 2018 Louisville Mayor Greg Fischer presented Ron with a Lifetime Achievement for Work in The Arts Award. In 2019 Ron was named Kentucky's Beat Poet Laureate and was also the first U.S. citizen to be named UNESCO's Tartu City of Literature Writer-in-Residence. He is co-founder and Chief of Poetics for Gonzofest Louisville. Outlaw Poet: The Legend of Ron Whitehead movie will be released by Storm Generation Films/Dark Star TV in 2021.

Joseph Fulkerson runs **Laughing Ronin Press** and is the author of six books. His most recent chapbook, ***A Six-pack for Chinaski*** was published by **Laughing Ronin Press.** He lives and works in the bourbon-soaked hills of Western Kentucky. **www.LaughingRoninPress.com https://fulkersonscorner.bigcartel.com**

Jonathan S Baker lives and works in Evansville, Indiana. There they have created a buffer shield of degenerates and perverts to protect their self from the harsh surrounding conditions. They are the author of multiple collections of poetry with ***It's Always Been Like This*** being the most recent release.

Sam Pink will kill your boss with one strike.
Twitter @sampinkisalive IG @sam_pink_art

Martin Appleby is a punk, poet, vegetarian, cider drinker from Hastings, England. He edits **Paper and Ink Literary Zine**, hosts **Punk and Poetry Podcast** and runs **Scumbag Press**. **www.scumbagpress.co.uk**

Isaac S. Hale is an American writer, researcher, and independent journalist. His creative works in surrealism include short stories and flash fiction, with a smattering of poetry here and there. He can be contacted through **Laughing Ronin Press.**

Dave Cullern is a poet, singer, podcaster and coffee roaster based in Hastings on the south coast of England. He has written two poetry ***collections (Modern Extremes and Poems About Fucking)***, a split chapbook ***(Fresh Words For Rotting Poems w/Martin Appleby)*** and has appeared in print and online via a number of small press publications. He can be contacted at **@fuckballads** on **IG** and **shamcityroasters@gmail.com**.

Victor Clevenger spends his days in a Madhouse and his nights writing poetry. Selected pieces of his work have appeared in print magazines and journals around the world; it has also been nominated for the Best of the Net Anthology and the Pushcart Prize. He is the author of several collections of poetry including ***Sandpaper Lovin'*** (Crisis Chronicles Press, 2017), ***A Finger in the Hornets' Nest*** (Red Flag Poetry, 2018), ***Corned Beef Hash By Candlelight*** (Luchador Press, 2019), and ***A Wildflower In Blood*** (Roaring Junior Press, 2020). Together with American poet John Dorsey, they run **River Dog**. He can be reached at: **crownofcrows@yahoo.com**

Tohm Bakelas is a social worker in a psychiatric hospital. He was born in New Jersey, resides there, and will die there. His poems have appeared in numerous journals, zines, and online publications. He has published 10 chapbooks. He runs **Between Shadows Press**.

Printed in Great Britain
by Amazon

38444384R00030